A Picnic

Written by Emma Lynch

Let's pack a picnic.

salad

jam

napkins

six baps

lemon fizz
in cans

melon

rug

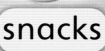

snacks

ham

1. Fill in

2. Fill the ham baps.
Fill the jam baps.

3. Pop the baps in bags.

4. Zip up the bags.
Pack the bags.

5. Cut up a melon into six bits. Pack the melon.

6. Toss a salad.

7. Pack the salad in the bag.

8. Pack the snacks and the lemon fizz in cans.

9. Get a rug to sit on.

10. Pack napkins to mop up mess.

11. Pick up the picnic bag.
Let's go.

13. Tuck in quick.
Yum, yum!

12. Pick a picnic spot.